10.29

A is for Anne:

Mistress Hutchinson

Disturbs the Commonwealth

Also by Penelope Scambly Schott

The Pest Maiden: A Story of Lobotomy (2004)

A is for Anne:

Mistress Hutchinson

Disturbs the Commonwealth

A Narrative Poem by Penelope Scambly Schott

A Turning Point Series Selection

Published by Turning Point
P.O. Box 541106
Cincinnati, OH 45254-1106

ISBN: 9781933456683
LCCN: 2007926462

Poetry Editor: Kevin Walzer
Business Editor: Lori Jareo

Visit us on the web at www.turningpointbooks.com

Cover Image: Acrylic painting by Penelope Scambly Schott based on Donald Gilligan's photo of the split rock near Anne's last home.

In loving memory of my father Elihu Schott
who helped to form my mind

Table of Contents

Anne Marbury Hutchinson, 1591-1643, was a highly vocal and influential religious leader in early Puritan Boston.

Because her independence of thought and speech threatened the civil authorities, she was convicted of heresy and banished from the colony of Massachusetts.

The Family of Anne Marbury Hutchinson

Bridget Dryden ---- Francis Marbury
|
|
Anne Marbury ----- William Hutchinson
(1591-1643) | (1586-1642)
|

Edward Hutchinson	(1613-1675)
Susannah Hutchinson	(1614-1630)
Richard Hutchinson	(1615-1682)
Faith Hutchinson	(1617-1652)
Bridget Hutchinson	(1619-1696)
Francis Hutchinson	(1620-1643)
Elizabeth Hutchinson	(1621-1630)
William Hutchinson	(1623-1631)
Samuel Hutchinson	(1624-1675)
Ann Hutchinson	(1626-1643)
Mary Hutchinson	(1628-1643)
Katherine Hutchinson	(1630-1643)
William Hutchinson	(1631-1643)
Susannah Hutchinson	(1633-1713)
Zuriell Hutchinson	(1636-1643)

Let your women keep quiet in the churches: for it is not permitted unto them to speak; but they are commanded to be under obedience as also saith the law.
—*I Corinthians* 14:34-35

A preaching woman and a crowing hen always come to a bad end.
—an English proverb

The government of this woman's Tongue hath bine a great Cause of this Disorder.
—Reverend John Wilson, in *A Report of the Trial of Mistress Anne Hutchinson before the Church in Boston*

Mistress Hutchinson, you are called here as one of those that have troubled the peace of the commonwealth and the churches here; you are known to be a woman that hath had a great share in the promoting and divulging of those opinions that are the cause of this trouble.
—Governor John Winthrop, in *A Report of the Trial of Mistress Anne Hutchinson before the Church in Boston*

This rose-bush, by a strange chance, has been kept alive in history: but whether it had merely survived out of the stern old wilderness...or whether, as there is fair authority for believing, it had sprung up under the footsteps of the sainted Anne Hutchinson... we shall not take upon us to determine.
—Nathaniel Hawthorne, in *The Scarlet Letter*

...here is the end and beginning of the story...

Years Later, Susannah Hutchinson Cole
Remembers the Death of her Mother in 1643

I do not think in English very well.

When Cole asked me to marry
him, I was still an Indian

and spoke just as they spoke
after they took me.

The tale they tell of killing my mother
gathers its reasons in telling:

how each season
the Whites came more and more,

how deer
flee from our forests,

and the arduous trial of hunger
falls heavy on the people.

Here I see her old face aglow
in the light

of the flaming house.

Mouth open wide,
she is greatly rejoicing.

In Adam's Fall
We sinned all.

A is a house, or else

it is a mouse house, or else

a mouse is up in our garret,

one little velvet gray mouse

over my own head   *squeak*

squeak

Anne Marbury is a Small Girl in Alford, Linconshire, England, Christendom

Here
is the center of the world

bounded by seas.
I am Anne.

Anne is me.
I paddle my hands

in the puddle
and I talk to the frogs.

There is mud on my hem. Thick black mud.

       Why
       am I always in trouble?

Reverend Francis Marbury is under House Arrest for Preaching against the Church of England

Papa's finger longer than my hand.
My older sisters learn their stitches,
and I, my letters. Our Queen reads,
so why not Anne?

Other fathers go about in the world,
but not mine. We sit in the parlor
picking out *A*'s: *A*dam. *A*braham.
*A*nne. *A*nne.

Papa teaches me names: Ann
is the mother of Virgin Mary; Ann
is Baby Jesus's own Granny; Ann
is Anne is me.

Mama beckons from the kitchen:
Small fingers to pluck the chicken.
Papa answers from the parlor:
We are busy now, I and Anne

Job feels the rod
Yet blesses God.

J is the Cross whereon Jesus died

with a little seat at the very bottom

where I sit with this pewter porringer

to catch His save-me-only-by-Grace

Blood. Mama says I eat too slowly

and please not to wave my spoon

in the air as if I were chasing moths.

Grace, I want to tell her. I chase

after Grace. I will be as good as

I can be, or He makes me.

My Two Primers

In the Dame School we have just one,
the Holy Scriptures, but here at home,
I have *two* books to read: Scripture
and Papa's Trial.
                    He likes to help me
point by point as I sound out his words.

We see the bishops are very naughty
but Papa is very wise. Sometimes
when he tricks the Bishop, we laugh,
sometimes out loud, or in our hearts.

I like how Papa can be funny, also
I like how he is always right. Christ
likes us smart as well as good.
                                Yes,
I do try to be good. I'm mostly good
at being smart.

My Father's Trial is my Second Primer

In which the Ecclesiastical Court of High Commission meets in the Consistory of Saint Paul's Cathedral on November 5, 1578

My father, the Reverend Francis Marbury, stands before his seated judges:

Bishop: *What have you to say to us?*

Papa: *Nothing but God save you.*

Bishop: *Nothing? Why you were wont to bark.*

Papa: *I come not to accuse but to defend, but because you urge me, I say the bishops of London are guilty of the death of as many souls as have perished by the unable ministers of their making.*

Bishop: *The proposition is false. If it were in Cambridge, it would be hissed out of the schools.*

Papa: *Then you had need to hire hissers.*

Recorder: *Marbury, use my Lord more reverently. I perceive your words are puffed up with pride.*

Papa: *Sir, I speak but truth to him. I reverence him so far as he is reverend, and I pray God to teach him to die.*

Bishop: *Have him to prison.*

Papa: *I am to go whither it pleaseth God. I pray God to forgive you.*

Bishop: *Thou takest upon thyself to be a preacher, but thou art a very ass, an idiot, and a fool. By my troth, I think he be mad.*

Papa: *Sir, I take exception against swearing judges. I praise God I am not mad, but sorry to see you so out of temper.*

>My Papa is never out of temper
>like Mama gets with me,

>not once ever.

The Big News of 1603

I am the husband and the whole Isle is my lawful wife;
I am the head and it is the body — James I

By the market place of Alford, they toll the bell.
Papa says Queen Bess is dead.

I know her bishops were popish, but I liked her dresses.

Maybe she'll go to Hell.

Now we will get King James.
He hates midwives and mystics in churches and kitchens.
He says: *The more Women, the more Witches.*

Well, shame on you, James.

I may only be twelve, but I'd witch you myself
with a willow switch.

Annie, calls my mother, *go stir the pot.* So I do as I'm told,
but I'd rather that I were a stirrer of souls.

Daughter of a Dissenter

I am my father's dearest scholar:

see how he leads me through deep waters.
Denied his parish, my father ravishes me

with argument of fiercest precision,
chapter and verse correctly quoted.

At the shore of the horizon,
my perishable soul

totters and slips.

        When will God know me?

Now I Read Scripture

alone. No one to pick out
meanings for me.

My father is dead:
an amputation in my brain.

Words I hold in my memory,
I hear in his voice. How

will I learn on my own?

I try to think:

Francis Marbury,
only a name. Today

the North Sea clouds
and the cold North Sea

are the same gray color.

> I open the cover
> of my father's Bible:
>
> Survival, Redemption,
> and Resurrection.
>
> Body and soul.
> How Papa's words
>
> will hold me.

Here Another Daughter Speaks Backwards and Forwards across the Years

This, the vastness of grief:
how it creeps into each day like a fresh loss.

Missing him breathing. Another daughter bereft.

Left alone
with a part of my mind formed to his masculine mode.

Whatever happens next, wherever I go from here,
my father will never know it.

But that doesn't matter

because I have become two people.
If I want to know what my dead father would think,

I can always summon the *him* in me.

Francis Marbury's Last Will and Testament

To each daughter and son:
two hundred pounds sterling,

the girls to remain with Mother
until marriage.

        But I at twenty-one
am old to marry. And plain

and much too tall. Of all
acceptable young men,

not one so tall or clean
as William Hutchinson.

Our reverends commend
the pleasures in marriage,

so why not? If generation
be the fate of man

and woman,

        Hey, nonny, no,
        as the old song goes,
        I'll do what I can.

Whales in the sea
God's voice obey.

V+V=W

How's that for a clever conceit?

If *V* is for *Vita,* my life + his life,

if whales meet deep in the sea,

if God's voice lives in my flesh,

I may just as well marry my Will.

William Hutchinson, merchant—

I could do worse.   He loves me

without question.   All the words

I need, I got from my dear father

or else from the Scriptures. Will

shall cherish my body and heart;

Besides, he has beautiful thighs.

I Like It Well

Mistress of my own home:
kitchen and gathering room

and the high, curtained bed
at the top of the stairs. Who said

it was duty? I grow in beauty
under his hands. To know

my husband as Eve knew Adam
as Rachel knew Jacob, as Mother,

Father. It's a wise God
devised this jointure of flesh.

        I applaud His gentle rod.

Here in our Curtained Bed, I Sin Not with my Tongue

Certain ignorant ministers, most distrustful of women,
always like to repeat

that by tongue of the Serpent, Eve was seduced,
and that *her* tongue seduced Adam.

> Yet I do not repent. My tongue is warm
> and wet. I can please a man.

Boy, Girl, Boy

Year after year, they arrive.

Between bearing my own
and midwifing for neighbors,

so little room.

Always at night, a knock.

Something inside me
ready to break.

I Am Much Troubled

Three small babes and pregnant,
I scarce attend my soul. Fiercely

I dissent from our vicar in Alford.
Must I recast myself a Separatist,

take up with poor unlettered folk?
So troubled am I in spirit,

I cannot bear it.

Twelve-month together, I know not
what to do. Why, God, do I weep?

Why cast myself down on this bed
and weep? Below in the warm kitchen,

Edward, Susannah and baby Richard,
barely weaned, clutch at the skirts

of my maidservant, calling *Mama*.

        I bolt the door.

        Under my starched
        bodice, my heart

        roars.

All Day I Fast and Pray

Show me, I pray Thee.

Rend the veil that hides Thy truth
from me.

My dry tongue sticks to my dry teeth.

I open my Bible at random: *2nd Epistle of John:*

> *He that denies Jesus Christ is come in the flesh,*
> *is a deceiver and antichrist.*

Which means?

God shines His voice at me:

> *He is the <u>antichrist</u> who doth not teach the new*
> *covenant.*

> *The new covenant is that which rests wholly upon the*
> *word of God as given in the Bible, and <u>not</u> on*
> *ordinances, forms, and ceremonies imposed by man.*

Clarity. Absolution.
The absolute ease of absolute faith.

I see it, I see it, how my soul is glowing.
Christ, I am saved and I know it.

> Let William come in from the shop.
> Let evening prayers begin.

Awake at Midnight

The moon on the roof
of the wellhouse

flares
like an angel's wing.

Is it Papist
to think so? No,

for God made the earth
and all its charms—

this unborn child
dancing in my womb

and our big bedstead
so warm.

My New Daughter Christened on August 14, 1617

As I am risen from my year of doubt,
so too I rise from childbed, as strong

or stronger than before: my daughter
perfectly made in the image of God,

if God were woman.

       I bundle her in Belgian lace
and good English flannel. Our family

walks to church all wreathed in sun;
under our feet, cobblestones glisten.

       This child shall be christened *Faith.*

Seeking a Teacher

Bread in my mouth.
Faith is a treasure

but my soul craves
wisdom too.

I am chasing
the pearls of the rain.

John Cotton of Saint Botolph's in the old town of Boston in Lincolnshire, England

Short, stout, scrawny blond hair,
the barest tuft of a beard—

not handsome, but once I heard
John Cotton preach, I saw

only the broad clear brow,
the delicate, sensuous lips,

divine comfort that drops
from his mouth. A calmness

of joy that brightens the heart,
each word certain.

When I listen to Mr. Cotton, I need
neither chasten nor bind my own,

sound, God-given mind.

The Great Comet of 1618

Don't tell me how it travels from east to west.
Don't call it a harbinger for pilgrims to sail west.

Can you show me any star that *doesn't* go west?

God speaks to me by revelation less ambiguous
than chatter in the market square.

> If my dear father were alive today,
> I know exactly what he'd say: *Piffle.*

> As I do too.

The Ride South to Saint Botolph's

From Alford to Boston, twenty-four miles:
just the distance of my needy soul.

I mount behind William, pillion,
my hands at his waist; warmth

throbs through his skin
to my very fingertips

like John Cotton's voice
will throb through my soul.

He doesn't preach to me of rituals
or earthly virtuous deeds.

Such cold doctrine of Works chills my soul.
And my husband thinks as I do.

Often we go to Boston. William and I ride
with no secrets between us.

        Today along the lazy river Witham,
        a rainy haze settles in rushes

        over white cattle egrets.

What I Make or Grow

Candles, bread,
soap, preserves,
beer, cured meats,
babies.

Syrups, decoctions
lotions, tonics
of simples and worts:

Feverfew to lower fever, lemon balm against melancholy,
borage for the heart, spearmint for digestion, sage for
memory, bugle against nightmares

Lady's mantle for conception, tansy to prevent
miscarriage, horehound to ease labor, betony for labor
pains, stinging nettle for breast milk, comfrey to heal
nursing sores

and did I say *babies*?

> Edward
> Susannah
> Richard
> Faith
> Bridget
> Francis
> Elizabeth
> William
> Samuel
> Ann
> Mary
> Katherine

> Will snores beneath our eiderdown;
> suppose I am again with child?

In 1630, the Plague Runs through Alford

It comes northeast from London
skipping and jumping and striking down
hither and yon.

I sprinkle the hall with ashes of roses.

The market closes. Shops are bare,
no stranger dares to enter town.
We leave silver coins in vinegar
inside the hollow stone at Miles Cross Hill,
hoping the farmers won't let us starve.

                    *

My first daughter, Susannah,
an eager sixteen and promised,
is taken from us.

What did I do wrong? I let her sing
with her sisters. God's mystery
perplexes.

Three weeks later, pretty Elizabeth gone.
No headstone, either one.
They who were burnt to stop contagion,
may their ashes in His everlasting grace,
rise, rise.

                    *

I will set no plague mark on our door:
— *Lord Have Mercy Upon Us* —

No sin of ours within struck down
my girls. But I used to pull my fingers
through the ringlets of Bessie's gold curls.
Was that *Vainglory?*

Lord, I worry.

Even as all returns to normal

Large crows crowd on roof peaks as
icicles melt and racing gutters overflow.

No more glutted rats in the High Street.
On Tuesday the town market reopens.

Under my wide skirts, this newest child
quickens. When I grow too big to ride

to Boston and back, then how to hear
my teacher's voice? How to feed my soul

with Mr. Cotton's wisdom? I will feel
the lack.

Now at the Court of High Commission
someone makes a complaint: *Cotton*

fails to ask the magistrates to kneel
when they take Communion.

Just where in holy text did Jesus Christ
demand such popish kneeling? Nowhere.

William cares more that the port silts
and prices for our wool decline.

> Even pregnant, I walk
> with a straight spine.

Bishop Laud, the Clothier's Son,

strikes down the nonconformists
one by one. Laud summons,

silences, removes all ministers
who resist false rites.

Mr. Cotton disappears by night,
shipping aboard the Griffin.

We go no more to St. Botolph's,
Will and I.

            The spirit within me

        starves
        and is throttled.

Mingle-Mangle

Go ahead. Hurl words
at my head.   My skull

bongs
like a bronze bell:

Heaven   Hell   Hell

Election or *Redemption?*
Justification or *Sanctification?*

Covenant of Works
or *Covenant of Grace?*

Now the ignorant
preach to the ignorant,

while all the misguided
are guided by fools.

But Christ has entered me;
I carry the seed of His truth

like a clean lens in my own mind.

Everything
shines clear to me:

the English clergymen are antichrists
who cling to the worldly proof of Works

where any hypocrite may seem *Elect.*

Give me ten minutes
face to face, and I'll know

for a fact
whether *you* have Grace.

Queen Esther comes in royal state
To save the Jews from dismal fate.

Q is for question. The perfect circle
dragging its damnable tail of doubt. How
to know one is saved? All last night, I sat
with a woman in labor, her infant breach
and hard to turn: in her pain she asked me,
Will I go to Hell? Hell is where the ministers
belong, those who teach her fear. *It is Love*
that will save us, I told the bleeding woman.

God Answers Me

Greatly I miss my father.

Now Reverend Cotton is sailing west,
no preacher left whom I can trust.

I must study and pray alone.
My Bible opens to *Isaiah*:

> *And though the Lord give you*
> *the bread of adversity and the water of affliction,*
>
> *yet shall not thy teachers be removed any more,*
> *but thine eyes shall see thy teachers.*

So I must follow Mr. Cotton.

Thank you, Lord,
for such direct instruction.

For Fear of Murder or Witchcraft, The English Church Forbids Midwives from Performing Emergency Infant Baptisms

Soon
will ghoulish *yeth-hounds* roam

the shadow-baited night,
those headless dogs,

pale homeless spirits
of unbaptized babes

raving and rambling
in the secret forest,

wailing,
wailing.

It freezes my blood.

        Please tell me,

        my good helpmeet Will,
        how soon, how soon

        can we sail?

Hosannas

Alas, we must wait another season.
But I am blessed with a new Susannah.

I have named her for her older sister
Susannah, whom I sorely miss.

Though I leave the ashes in Alford,
now her name will sail with us

across the ocean
to God's new kingdom in this world.

Unpleasant Weeks Aboard the Griffin

After twenty-one years in the same house,
we've put our lives in trunks and sacks,

leaving the curtained bed behind
to sleep in cold arms of an untracked sea —

but our ship knows the way: blessed vessel
that just a year ago

brought Mr. Cotton to New England.

Our voyage is made worse
by Governor Winthrop's hundred cows

plus chickens, pigs, and geese
who squawk and reek and bellow down below,

and though the deck hands flush the deck
daily with vinegar made of beer,

it stinks.

We hear sermons every day. Yesterday,
one Reverend Symmes spoke contrary

to what I know. This morning on deck,
I raise the point. He takes it amiss.

I am rebuked:

> *For the man is not of the woman,*
> *but the woman is of the man.*

I grant him this: he's read his *1st Corinthians*.
Let him roar like the cattle. I grant him

nothing more.

Arrival

Almost two months aboard ship
and nothing to do

but trouble Mr. Symmes:
What would you say, I ask, *if we should be*

at New England within these three weeks?
And here we are. September 18, 1634,

auspicious day. Mr. Cotton comes to the dock
and leads us to the new town, its lumber

a raw yellow. I follow through mud, glad
to be at last so near the teacher of my soul.

I am only somewhat distressed
when dear Mr. Cotton stands up tall

to whisper into my ear:
Here it be tactful to hold one's tongue.

> The uncobbled street looks shabby and mean,
> and the earth seems to lean beneath my feet.

I Try to be Glad We Have Come

Back home I heard the setting praised
as advantageous to the colonists:

> *It being a neck and bare of woods,*
> *they are not troubled with three great annoyances:*
> *of Wolves, Rattle-snakes and Mosquitoes.*

Indeed, I see no wolves. The children run
to their older brother who has been here a year.

I hold baby Susannah tightly under my shawl,
though the air is not cold.

Tomorrow they will start to build our house.
In barrows they trundle the window glass

we brought from home.

> So far across the sea, burnt bones
> of my dead daughters.
>
> I lean toward a passing barrow:
> the wrapping straw smells of Alford.

Mr. Hutchinson is Made a Deacon in the Church

Dear, respectable Will was accepted promptly,
so why not I?

Because aboard ship I slighted, says Symmes,
a minister of God.

Such a long voyage, and I was expected
to keep my mouth shut?

Here on land, I am watched with suspicion
and asked questions: what do I believe

about this and that? Many weeks pass;
they are satisfied at last:

She holds nothing different from us.

        Dearest Christ Almighty, what
        a preposterous

        fuss.

Very Early in the Morning

Indians and sailors
walk our street,

neither greatly
improved by drink.

The Indians stalk
like tall cats

passing our garden.
Good morning, I say.

They don't look back.

        My children gawk.

Each Monday Evening, in the Big Chair

I sit before the gathered women
and clarify the Sunday sermon.

I repeat and review and re-explain,
I entertain questions.

They all seem pleased to come—
they travel so seldom from home.

Some of these same women
I have assisted in childbed.

Each week, more women.

> Parched hearts
> drink at the fountain of Christ.

White Meats

Family supper we serve mild white meats:
bread and butter, cheese or eggs, and milk.

Spice comes in the meetings afterward: talk
of Reverend Wilson's confusions, and where
the Boston church is wrong.

Aristocratic young Governor Vane attends,
and a throng besides. I speak clearly
and explain what I can.

Back in Alford I spoke so, but not to so many.
The women came first, and now the men.

Such shoving for place.

We make and study distinctions
until what was hidden is plain.

The words swell on my tongue unbidden;

> then afterward I bed with Will
> who says I spoke well.

On the Edge of Wilderness

Succotash, pumpkin, samp;
for lack of flour I bake no bread:

all is molasses and Indian corn
and, though we scorn them,

lobsters and mussels. How like
the savages, tussling with shells.

Here on the edge of wilderness,
no matter the larder be spare:

it's a rich dish for my spirit
so long as John Cotton is near;

his voice swells with conviction
and I love to listen.

        Though my good husband is not
        so zealous as I, he need never

        be jealous. Marriage flowers
        in my justified blood.

Now Also on Thursday Nights

An ever larger meeting. They spill
from parlor to kitchen.

So many listeners. I am sure
of myself in my husband's chair.

Again the handsome Vane attends
to hear me explain and expound.

Were I not humble, I'd fain be proud.
No, I amend my words;

                    it is God

who makes the truth so plain,
who fans the Flame so loud.

                    Ardor. Ardor.

Private Interrogation at the Home of Mr. Cotton, October 25, 1636

Is Boston too small for more than one opinion?
If I am not *with* them, must I be *against* them?

All I demand is the right to speak what I think.

Instead they summon me here by night
for secret conversation.

With a kind of desperation, they query:

Do I truly believe only my teacher Cotton
and my brother-in-law Wheelwright preach
correctly the Doctrine of Grace?

How can I lie to their faces? I tap
my foot on the swept floor.

Answer the question directly, instructs Mr. Peters.
We come for plain dealing and telling you our hearts.

Thus I answer: *It is true, there is a wide difference
between you and Mr. Cotton.*

Cotton gets nervous. *I am sorry you put comparisons
between my ministry and theirs.*

I raise the palms of my hands, as if to show them
nothing hidden. *I find the difference.*

What plainer defense can I make? The saucy girl
who dwells in my skin is aching to give them

a good hard shaking.

    Later, after the moon is down,
    they creep to me one at a time, each asking,

    Is it _me_ you take to task?

    If they won't like my answers, why do they
    ask?

Now They Think to Spy on My Meetings

Tonight in the crush of the room,
I see faces of women I don't trust.

Who told them to come?

Mr. Winthrop and his cabinet
of narrow believers

think they are sanctified,
but they are not *Elect*.

Let them try to catch me out:
This evening I spout the Bible

word for word.

        Let them listen.
        Let them sneak back to Winthrop

        or tattle to Wilson.
        They will have heard nothing

        suspect.

Zaccheus, he
Did climb the tree
His Lord to see.

Z is a barred gate I will not pass.

Zuriell, my *Rock of God*, shall be my last.

Here at midway through my fifth decade,

arrives this miniature man-child, his toes

in their perfect rows. May this boy thrive.

May he reach manhood in a true church

above Mr. Winthrop's uninspired works.

My breasts droop and my womb is tired.

My Brother-in-Law John Wheelwright is Censured

It started well enough.   Our Boston congregation
chose him, but Winthrop and Wilson posted him

elsewhere.

(I wonder Mr. Cotton didn't speak to keep him.)

That was last fall. This January, all was turmoil.
Between war on the Pequots and quarrels of doctrine,
no one agreed.

Therefore a Fast Day was declared;

first Mr. Cotton spoke, and then my brother
Wheelwright prophesied:

> *When enemies to the truth oppose the way of God,*
> *we must lay load upon them, we must kill them*
> *with the word of the Lord.*
> >   *And should this cause*
> *a combustion in Church and Commonwealth, so be it,*
> *for did not Christ come to send fire upon the earth?*

Oh, yes, there is fire:
Winthrop and Wilson, mightily angered,
have censured him for *Sedition and Contempt.*

And now those puffed up fools are waiting for him
to recant.

As if the word of the Lord could be taken back.

Anne Bradstreet, Poet and Daughter to Thomas Dudley, Deputy Governor of the Massachusetts Bay Colony, Thinks about Anne Hutchinson

She frightens me, this pious scholar I once so greatly admired.
In the years I failed to conceive, I looked at her many children
and assumed she was blessed and therefore good.

I am safe up here in Ipswich: no rabble tangles with doctrine.
At night while she fornicates with her compliant husband,
my own husband and father must board on business in town.

My babies sleep. Hush. Hush. I have latched the shutters.
In this cold rain, nobody wanders about. Nobody will watch
how I hide in the flame of a candle, daring to prattle on paper.

This night so damp and my fingers cramped;
how women must pay for their brains.

The Great Debate in Boston

Assuredly,

no one will be redeemed
by ignorance or games.

Hoops and hopscotch
in the dusty road,

the village children
like miniature adults

play at naming faults
and being saved,

seeming to understand
nothing

about how grace is given
unearned.

Grace or Works?
they shriek.

       It becomes a contest:
       Works or Grace?

A Harsh Season

Is it not enough to deliver their babies,
treat their diseases, comfort their souls?

Must I also agree with fools?   Clouds
blow in from many directions. Look:

the weather vane spins like a demon.

The Hutchinsons' Brother-in-Law John Wheelwright Is Banished from the Colony

What could I do but write a petition?
Seventy-five good men signed.

And now the tale of dirty tricks:
When they held the General Election,
several of our deputies were never notified.

These things don't happen by chance.

Cambridge Common: May 17, 1637.
I wasn't there, of course, but I've been told.

Young Governor Vane calling the court to order,
trying to read our petition for Wheelwright.

Imagine the shouting. What happened next,
I can't imagine, except I know:

plump Mr. Wilson climbs an oak tree
and orders the vote for deputies.
Winthrop seconds.

Vane says again he will read the petition.
Out of order, rules Winthrop.

Out of power is Vane. And Winthrop back in office

where the court has waited until now,
the hard end of November, to banish my brother-in-law

into the wilderness.

The days so grim. So short.

The Pequot Indian War Temporarily Outweighs
the Theological War

With Vane out of office and Wilson made chaplain,
the men of our faction refuse to enlist.

Meanwhile Winthrop must smile on Rhode Island
hoping that banished Roger Williams

will keep his Indians out of the war. Remind me,
what was Reverend Williams banished for

if not the same thing I am doing? I will not be
as soon forgiven.

> Perhaps in Heaven women get equal voice.
> There, the Son will reveal His choice.

And Now Comes the Coup

Suddenly our petition is termed *seditious libel.*

Our list of signers is now transformed
to a list of public enemies.

Authorities punish all who signed,
saying they *disturb the public peace.*

My husband's brother is jailed, fined forty pounds,
and he and many others disenfranchised.

They silence numerous of our friends
upon pain of banishment.

But it gets worse:

Despite the risk of Indians and beasts,
despite the winter need for meat,

some fifty-eight grown men are, by command,
disarmed.

Winthrop and Wilson confiscate *all such guns,*
pistols, swords, powder, shot and match

as they shall have in their custody, upon pain
of ten pounds for every default.

Only those who acknowledge their sin
to two magistrates may keep their arms.

What?
Does our Governor Winthrop fear for his life?

Twenty families follow Mr. Wheelwright north.
Does Winthrop feel safe yet?

I study my face in the back of a spoon:
just what is this great threat?

Why I, Governor Winthrop, Am Increasingly Troubled for Our Colony

Nobody calls me *fool*. I know too well what stows
aboard each returning ship:

gossip and tales.

If news of this local commotion should reach London,
we face heavy consequences:

our whole Massachusetts Bay Charter could be
preemptively withdrawn.

We are the City on the Hill. We are the city
on the hill. We are the city. We are. Therefore

we must keep our own house in order. Why
does Mister Hutchinson fail to control his wife?

I Never Knew I Was So Powerful

Yet, having no gun, no sword,
nor masculine organ,

I still have words.

Imagine if I had been pretty.

They Found Harvard College to Train Obedient Clergy

Look how they try to argue back:

a pile of books and a pocket of cash
left to the authorities by a sick man,

one timbered building, a thatch roof,
and they dare to call this a college?

I call it their fountain of propaganda.

Have they been to Oxford or Cambridge?
Do they know how a human heart and mind

can be blessed with questions?

They never question their Biblical exegesis;
instead they teach Theology

as if it were plane geometry, deriving proofs
of what they already believe.

                                Or maybe
they don't even believe what they teach;

maybe it's just a convenient tool
for fooling the people

or keeping them under control,
as if Conformity conferred Security.

                    I thought we were the *common* wealth
                    of Massachusetts. I thought each man

                    had value. Each *man* and each *woman*.

Wilson's Sermon Attacks Me

Recently at Watertown

there was (in view of diverse witnesses)
a great combat between a mouse and snake

and after a long fight, the mouse prevailed
and killed the snake. The snake is the Devil,

the mouse is brought hither by God
to dispossess the Devil, preaches Wilson.

    Well, Mister Wilson,
    am I Snake or Mouse?

He cavils, this so-called Reverend. Truly,
Wilson disgusts me. What does *he* know?

    He wouldn't know Grace
    if it pinched his fat nose.

What our Ministers Seem to Think:

that the open mouth of a woman
is the womb of foul Error

or:

that the womb of a woman
is a vile mouth of the Devil

      Such woman-hating,
      chowder-brained fools.

      After love-making,
      I have sniffed myself
      upon my husband's flesh:

      a whiff of flounder, maybe,
      but never sulphur.

Freedom in the New World

This morning a lynx
slinks past our door, and a bear

in the root cellar sleeps, musk
skunk-thick, masking

the scent of rotting apples. I know
that animals do not have souls,

not even this bear with her cubs;
still I prop the root cellar door

open
in order not to trap her.

> Later among berry bushes,
> she harvests with dexterous tongue;
>
> how mobile her shining black lips.

Imposition of the Alien Act

First they tried to ban my meetings:

how can they call them *disorderly* when all we do
is talk of Christ?

Now State and Church flaunt their power as one:
to say who stays or not in Massachusetts.

Where once we were refuge, we make refugees,
sending new arrivals hence.
                              On the 12th of July,
my husband's brother comes from England,
and gladly we rush to the dock to see him,

but the new law gets there first:

*No one may stay here for more than three weeks
without permission.*

Hutchinsonians they call those who take my part.

Look at my raw hands: these are not the hands
of a scholar or heretic. *Midwife, washerwoman,
soap maker.*

I wonder why they are so afraid of me. Winthrop
thinks I usurp his place.

                    And who am I
                    but a scrubber of children's dirty faces?

Secret Burial: October 17, 1637

A most unfortunate lying-in:

poor Mary Dyer, the milliner's wife, two months pre-term
births a stillborn girl—after a manner of speaking,

but I hope never again to see such a deformed thing.

Midwife Jane Hawkins, ignorant though she be,
chases all but me from the room.

Late at night we knock on Reverend Cotton's window,
asking, what, in God's name, should we do?

He comes with a shovel, agrees the thing should be
concealed to protect Mary from blame.

Now it is buried in a secret place where neither hog nor dog
nor any other beast may find it.

Whether such a creature, had it lived, would be fit to baptize,
I am not wise enough to guess.

    Mr. Cotton won't say *no* or *yes*.

Trials on Earth

How has this come to pass?

All I have done is walk the path
of God's own truth.

If earthly authority falls into error,
must I not be a carrier

of correction? Was Daniel
scared of lions? Then why

shall I be frightened?

My First Trial by the General Court: November 2, 1637

Two Excerpts from the Transcript: Day One

Exhibit A:

Governor Winthrop: *Mistress Hutchinson, you are called*
   here as one of those that have troubled the peace of the
   commonwealth and the churches here. You have said things
   prejudicial to the ministers and you have held meetings
   at your house that have been condemned.

Me: *I am called here to answer before you, but I hear no*
   things laid to my charge.

Winthrop: *I have told you some already and more I can tell*
   you.

Me: *Name one, Sir.*

Winthrop: *Have I not named some already? We do not*
   mean to discourse with those of your sex.

         Well, of course not.
         What ought I expect?

Exhibit B:

Me: *What law have I broken?*

Winthrop: *The Law of God and of the State.*

Me: *In what particular?*

Winthrop: *In this among the rest, whereas the Lord says honor thy father and thy mother.*

Me: *Eh, Sir, in the Lord.*

Winthrop: *You have dishonored the commonwealth, Mistress Hutchinson. What say you to your weekly public meetings?*

Me: *There were such meetings before I came.*

Winthrop: *There were private meetings indeed. Yours are of another nature. But answer by what authority you uphold them.*

Me: *By Titus 2, where the elder women are to teach the younger.*

Winthrop: *So we allow you to do. Privately.*

Me: *Will you please to give me a rule against it, and I will yield.*

Winthrop: *You must have a rule for it.*

Me: *And why do you call me to teach the Court?*

Winthrop: *See how your argument stands. Priscilla, with her husband, took Apollo home to instruct him privately. Therefore Mistress Hutchinson without her husband may teach sixty or eighty.*

Me: *I call them not. But if they come to me, I may instruct them.*

Winthrop: *Yet you show not a rule.*

Me: *I have shown you two places in Scripture.*

Winthrop: *But neither of them will suit your practice.*

Me: *Must I show my name written therein?*

And wasn't this last rejoinder worthy
of my father?

I place one hand over my mouth
to stifle a laugh.

Regret at Night

They think I will back down tomorrow:
repent, recant, revise, restate, rethink
my answers.   They think I will regret.

Am I making a mistake?

Can an ocean flow into a lake?
Will a stone roll uphill?
Does the rain regret falling?

Or Christ undo His covenant with me?

First, above all, I must guard my soul.

But how to care for my young children?
At this late hour, I hunger to touch them.

My thoughts float in circles.

I remind my husband not to forget
mint for Susannah's sore throat.

        And yet, I may still win.

        And yet

My First Trial by the General Court

Further Excerpts from the Transcript: Day Two

<u>Exhibit C:</u>

Me: *I shall give you the ground of what I know to be true. The Lord gave me to see that those who did not teach the new covenant had the spirit of antichrist, and ever since, He has let me see which was the clear ministry and which the wrong.*

The Lord revealed himself to me, sitting upon a throne of justice and all the world appearing before him. The Lord spoke this to me.

An assistant to the Court: *How do you know it was the Lord who spoke to you?*

Me: *How did Abraham know that it was God that bid him offer his son?*

Deputy Governor Thomas Dudley: *By an immediate voice.*

Me: *So to me by an immediate revelation.*

Dudley: *How! an immediate revelation.*

Me: *By the voice of His own spirit to my soul.*

Blessed be the Lord who gives me His word.
Having Christ in my heart, I will not swerve.

Exhibit D:

Me: *You have power over my body but the Lord Jesus hath
    power over my body and soul; and if you go on in this
    course, you will bring a curse upon you and your posterity. The
    mouth of the Lord hath spoken it.*

Winthrop: *I am persuaded that the revelation she brings
    forth is delusion.*

Most of the court: *We all believe it. We all believe it.*

Winthrop: *Therefore if it be the mind of the court that Mrs.
    Hutchinson shall be banished, let them hold up their hands.*

Most members of the court raise their hands.

Winthrop: *Mistress Hutchinson, the sentence of the court
    you hear is that you are banished from out of our
    jurisdiction as being a woman not fit for our society, and
    are to be imprisoned till the season be fit for the court to
    send you away.*

Me: *I desire to know wherefore I am banished.*

Winthrop: *Say no more. The court knows wherefore and is
    satisfied.*

            Thus I must follow my father to prison.

            I am neither the first nor the last
            to be punished for creating division.

Imprisoned at Roxbury until the Season Be Fit for my Exile

Even now I bethink me
of Papa. How unabashed

before the Queen's assembled Bishops
he stood, and would not dissemble

or give in.
I remember his retort:

> *Then you had need to hire hissers.*

So the Bishop sends him to prison.

And I, his daughter, here in Roxbury
where nobody wishes me well.

> *Papa, this is Anne calling.*
> *Though pride comes, they say,*
>
> *before a fall, please, Papa,*
> *be proud*
>
> *of me.*

Four Winter Months Confined to an Upstairs Room in the Roxbury House of Joseph Weld, Brother to Reverend Thomas Weld who Hates Me

Seven young children at home
and these holy men keeping me

from them.

Here I have nothing to do.
Either I am pregnant, or else

unwell. Something feels wrong.
All day long, I am heartsick

and lonely and bored. No woman
speaks me a word. Only

the strictest ministers come,
in pairs for mutual protection,

to berate, debate or ask
quite tenderly what I believe.

At first,
I am eager to greet them,

glad to descend to the parlor
where we dissect Scripture.

> Then it gets clearer:
> they are trying to trap me

> in what they call *Errors*.

My Second Trial: March 16, 1638

Day One: the morning on which I am Adamant

Ill as I am, I find it hard
to stand so long in this chilly meeting house
as they read out, slowly, each of twenty-nine so-called
Errors.

Clerk: *It is desired by the church, Sister Hutchinson, that*
you express whether this be your opinion or not.

Me: *If this be error, then it is mine and I ought to lay it down.*
If it be truth, it is not mine but Christ Jesus and then I am
not to lay it down

We go at it endlessly, hour upon hour and point by point.
These points, among others, I strongly defend:

That a man is united to Christ by the work of the Spirit
upon him and not by any act of his own.

That God loves a man no better for any holiness in
him, and no less if he is unholy.

That a minister who lacks this new light is unable to
teach.

That a man may have all graces, and yet lack Christ.

But other views they assign me were never mine.

Me: *I did not hold diverse of these things I am accused of,*
but only asked a question.

Reverend Shepard: *The vilest errors that ever were brought into the church were brought by way of questions.*

       Hah. Just what I thought:
       no one here is supposed to think.

       At their new college, there will be no debate;
       nothing taught but answers they want

       to uphold their state.

My Second Trial: March 16, 1638

Day One: the afternoon on which Mr. Cotton Abandons Me

Mr. Cotton turns his face to me, and his heart against me.

Mr. Cotton: *I have often feared the height of your Spirit and being puffed up with your own parts.*

> *Your opinions fret like a gangrene and spread like a leprosy, and infect far and near, and will eat out the very bowels of religion.*

He turns to the women's side of the meetinghouse:

> *Let me say this to you all, let not the good you have received from her make you accept everything she says. For, you see, she is but a woman. Many unsound and dangerous principles are held by her.*

> *If you have drunk in any evil poison, make speed to vomit it up again and to repent of it.*

And now he reproaches me:

> *Consider how many poor souls you have misled.*

My teachings, he says, will cause Antinomian excess,

> *and all promiscuous and filthy coming-together of men and women without distinction or relation of marriage will necessarily follow.*

And though I have not heard that you have been
unfaithful to your husband, yet that will follow upon it.

How dare Mr. Cotton address such words
to me?
How can he?

I who have birthed fifteen children
and known only one man.

My Trial is Recessed for Six Days

In the time God took to create our world,
I gyrate between fury and exhaustion.

My sometime friend Cotton advises
Be mild. But I guess how it will end.

William has gone ahead to build us
another house. I refuse to grieve.

Someday we shall live forever
in a better world than this.

I do know that. Only
sometimes

I forget.

My Second Trial: March 22, 1638

Day Two: the morning on which I Waver

Me: *I desire to speak one word before you proceed. I would
forbear, but by reason of my weakness I fear I shall not
remember it when you have done.*

Cotton: *You have leave to speak.*

Me: *All that I would say is this, I did not hold any of these
things before my imprisonment.*

*I spoke rashly and unadvisedly. I do not allow the slighting of
ministers, nor of the Scriptures, nor anything that is set
up by God.*

*My judgment is not altered though my expression
alters.*

Reverend Symmes: *I should be glad to see any humiliation
in Mistress Hutchinson. I fear these are no new things
but she believed them before.*

Cotton: *I think we are bound upon this ground to remove her
from us, seeing she prevaricates in her words.*

Deputy Governor Dudley: *And for her recantation, her
repentance is only on a piece of paper. Whether it was
written by her or she had help, I know not. But her repentance
is not in her countenance.*

Now I am ashamed.

Why did I listen to Mr. Cotton and try
to appease them?

I have been too eager to please him.

What's done is done.   Let it come.

My Second Trial: March 22, 1638

Day Two: the afternoon on which I am Cast Out

Reverend Peter: *You have stepped out of your place: You
have rather been a Husband than a Wife, and a Preacher
than a Hearer, and a Magistrate than a Subject.*

Wilson: *She is a dangerous instrument of the Devil.*

*The misgovernment of this woman's tongue has been a
great cause of this disorder. We would sin against God if
we did not put away from us so evil a woman, guilty of
such foul deeds.*

*Therefore in the name of our Lord Jesus Christ and in
the name of the church, I do cast you out, and in the name of
Christ, I do deliver you up to Satan that you may learn no
more to blaspheme, to seduce and to lie.*

*Therefore I command you as a Leper to withdraw yourself out
of the Congregation; that as formerly you have despised and
contemned the Holy Ordinances of God, so you may now have
no part in them nor benefit by them.*

The sky turns half-violet and the room
goes dark.

And then, sharply, I am strong again.

I Stride Out with my Shoulders Stiff

Many hope to see me trip.

A woman hisses with bitter lips:
The Lord sanctify this unto you,

as if I were some bad child needing correction.

I almost spit in her face:
The Lord judges not as man judges.
Better to be cast out of the church than to deny Christ.

The woman retreats and lowers her eyes.

> Now a friend comes up beside me
> and her warm arm slips into mine:

> brave, kind Mary Dyer.

As runs the Glass,
Man's life doth pass.

G is for God Who has never failed me,

Who always offers a small way home. Truly

I believe, all that befalls me has been foretold,

and God will keep me safe. Just as He closed

the jaws of the lions, I shall not be consumed.

Though I walk among wild beasts of the forest,

though I cross over rivers in full flood, yet God

will bring me through unscathed. Let the false

church of Massachusetts look to itself with fear.

The Exhumation of Mary Dyer's Miscarriage

Question: *Who is that woman?*
Answer: *She is the woman who had the monster.*

How did anyone find out?
We buried the corpse by lantern light in a hidden place.

Just as I leave,
Governor Winthrop orders the grave dug up.

Here he reports what he claims they found:

>*It was so monstrous and misshapen as has scarce
>been heard of. It had no head but a face, which stood
>so low upon the breast, as the ears, which were like
>an ape's grew upon the shoulders.*

>*The breast and back was full of sharp spines.*

>*The arms and hands were as other children's, but
>instead of toes it had on each foot three claws with
>talons.*

>*Upon the back it had two great holes like mouths, and
>in each of them stuck out a piece of flesh.*

>*It had no forehead but four horns, two of which were
>more than an inch long, hard, and sharp.*

Not so. I think Mr. Winthrop was hoping for Satan.
But there were no spines. No talons.
Certainly no horns.

>It was a sad little creature.
>Or two creatures half born.

Thy life to mend,
God's Book attend.

B is for Banishment. For my breasts
heavy in the fifth month, womb distended,
the taste of vomit in my mouth, but not yet
the flutter of life. From time to time, I bleed.
I can tell no one. Not my young children as
we walk six days through the frozen mire of
early April, between snow and thaw. Weary
Susannah, barely five, reaches for my hand.

B is for Bridge, I tell Susannah. I take
her cold hand as we step on this fallen log
to cross the swollen stream. Zuriell clings
to my neck. I tell the children and adults,
the whole muddy procession, how my heart
is chanting *HOME*, how God preserves us.
My wet toes have finally stopped burning.

Our New Home

William rushes to meet us at the edge
of the marsh.

He and the other men have been busy
felling trees.

After the harsh journey, I am grateful
even for a house that is not yet a house.

The first night, we sleep in the cellar hole.
I am still cold.

But the town is platted, the fields laid out.
We have been allotted good land

and our new walls rise.

What have we lost by leaving Boston?
Oppression and lies.

This Most Unfortunate Lying-In

My belly keeps rising
but will not quicken.

Something inside me
sickens.

Whatever it is
slides from me—

slips
like frogs' eggs

in brown jelly,

dripping
between my legs:

great clots
and lesser

dotting
this tin vessel.

Mr. Clarke, Physician of Aquidneck, Rhode Island, Writes to Governor Winthrop of Boston

An immoderate discharge from her womb
was brought to light and I was called to see it:

Innumerable distinct bodies in the form of a globe,
so confusedly knit together by so many several strings

so that it was impossible to number, much less to discern
from whence every string did fetch its original,

they were so snarled one within another.
The small globes I likewise opened,

and perceived the matter of them to be partly wind
and partly water. The lumps were twenty-six or twenty-seven,

distinct and not conjoined together, six as great as my fist,
the smallest the bigness of the top of my thumb,

and two, which differed from the rest, like liver or congealed
blood. There came no secundine or afterbirth.

The globes were round things, included in the lumps,
about the bigness of a small Indian bean

and like the pearl in a man's eye.

> Doctor Clarke, is nothing private.
> Now they will gloat in Boston.
>
> Must you glut John Winthrop
> who loves to hate me?

The Poet Anne Bradstreet Hears the News
When her Husband Simon Returns from Boston

It must have been hard enough to leave her house—
in each clothespress or cupboard, lavender sachets
or lemon balm or the scent of a child's white skirts.

And then to traverse a wilderness, heavy in the belly,
slow-footed, and clutching a frightened child's hand,
to arrive among new-hewn timbers and shaving curls,

no roof yet. Then to lose what never was a babe.
Thirty globules for her thirty doctrinal errors? Men
will say what men will say, and it won't be kind. How

can a man be so blind? I don't need to tell Simon,
but tonight I imagine I might have been her friend.

Preparing my Spring Garden in Aquidneck, Rhode Island

Tansy and sage come back;
parsley does not.

How far away old England seems
on this new raw shore.

Memories always come back;
the dead do not.

But see how the living can heal
from a difficult year:

had I not been carrying that growth,
would I have spoken better?

Sometimes I rethink what I told them;
mostly I don't.

Father's soul floating over Boston
would have approved.

But who are these three figures
striding up my path?

> *From whom do you come,* I call out,
> *and what is your business?*

> and I straighten up, still holding
> my sharpened hoe.

February 1640: Governor Winthrop, Still Hoping I Will Recant, Has Sent a Delegation from Boston to Aquidneck

Me: *From whom do you come and what is your business?*

Delegation: *We are come in the name of the Lord Jesus from the Church of Christ at Boston.*

Me: *There are lords many and gods many, but I acknowledge but one Lord. Which Lord do you mean?*

Delegation: *We are come in the name of but one Lord, and that is God.*

Me: *Then so far we agree. Where we do agree, let it be set down.*

Delegation: *We have a message to you from the Church of Christ in Boston.*

Me: *I know no church but one. For your church, I will not acknowledge it any church of Christ.*

Here our three unwelcome visitors give up on me and trudge off to bother my husband, my dearest, dearest Will.

William: *I am more nearly tied to my wife than to the church; she is a dear saint and servant of God.*

> At this point, Mr. Winthrop's delegation must turn around and head back to Boston in the snow.
>
> I am troubled they came and relieved when they go.

The Death of William at Age 56

Not two days would pass, but he pressed his chest against me,
his loins to my loins, and we were conjoined.

He was always a strong man, hoisting lumber or bolts of cloth.
In Alford, in Boston, even here in Aquidneck, he prospered.

I knew he was old but I never believed he would leave me.
William, Father, Cotton, all my men now vanished or turned.

Only Governor Winthrop
pursues me:

I am still too close to Massachusetts and its church.
I want to march far into the forest, that fire of green.

        The horizon grows dark. I had not thought
        there were so many, many stars.

I have Quit Rhode Island

I am settled here north of the Dutch on a little farm
not much above Bronk's land, close to Pelham Bay.

It is quiet, so quiet, that the man whom I hired
to build us this house said he was scared

of eyes that hide in the woods.

We live by a small river remote from neighbors.
If Winthrop gloats, I will never know it.

Behind the house is a hill with a split rock
where my children like to pick berries.

I teach them their letters and prayers.

        I am as old as my father in the year he died.

        Sometimes Indians drink from our well.
        All, I hope, will be well.

In Adam's fall
We sinned all.

A is a house. Look at the roof,
my little Zuriell, how it rises so steeply.

Look at the loft where your big sisters

sleep on their pallets under the eaves.

Here, let me help you hold the chalk:

two lines down, one across. Now what

comes next?

Anne at the Edge of this Life

What does it come to,
this poor world? Sometimes

God's Word
hides.

My tongue lies quiet
in the trench of my mouth,

curled to my front teeth.
I no longer preach.

I am pregnant with belief
and ready to be born

or to die.

> Three nights I have dreamed
> the same dream:
>
> *that the soul is nothing but light.*

Must All Governors be So Foolish?

1

The Dutch governor Willem Kieft,
for fear of Wild men,

attacks a sleeping village, murders
them all, even small children

curled up on furs.

Report of the massacre
will spread among the bands.

2

As muskrats dig in the bank,
as deer browse the meadow,

as fish flicker in the river,

how will the Indians
refrain from asking:

*who are these strangers
hammering trees?*

There is *one* cure.

Black Bear in my Garden

I dream I am dreaming: the huge hinge of her jaw,
the deep black maw into which I am falling.

My Dutch neighbors warn us of Indians and tell us
to leave. I am not young enough to start again.

> The bear's wet tongue is pink as
> the tongue of a babe, and soft as
> moss.

from the published account of Governor Winthrop

... But Mistress Hutchinson, being weary of Rhode Island or rather the island weary of her, departed to live under the Dutch in a place called by sea-men Hell-Gate.

There the Indians set upon them and slew her and all her family, save one girl-child that escaped. Some write that the Indians did burn her to death with fire, her house and all that belonged to her.

Therefore is God's hand the more apparently seen ...

What Susannah Can Remember Later

First they put the cow in the house,
and big mama sow with her seven shoats.

And my mother came to the door and asked why.
And the warriors all made a sound in their throats.

And they looked at the ground and up high
in the trees. And they sang the song about fire

before they lit the thatched roof. She stood
unmoving in the doorway and prayed aloud.

Welcome me, Christ, for I know I am saved.

Her hair caught. In the gleam of the flames
she became as beautiful as a shooting star.

Mother, you have joined the Great Mother
and every night I know where you are.

*

Postscript: The Lost Hornbook

geese are flying, our band comes to the bay
        my family is fishing

children run among rushes   and up the hill
there is a rock   there is a split rock
below the rock   a place she used to know
          that girl

that girl with the white skin who is no more me
leaves the other children   digs among ashes

beside what is left of a chimney,
a kind of paddle made of animal horn
with signs   with many strange signs:

S is a small grass snake   his green back
       with a yellow stripe down

      J is a fish hook

     U is a basket for carrying clams

    X is the stitches I make with sinew in deer hides

         Wait. I remember.
S is a girl whose first Mama called her *Susannah*

A is like a house. Here is the roof.
Inside is a mother   speaking Truth.
Her name is *Anne.*

* * *

Some Key Dates in the Life of Anne Marbury Hutchinson

1591 (July) Anne Marbury born in Alford, England

1611 Death of Anne's father the Reverend Francis Marbury

1612 Anne Marbury marries William Hutchinson

1630 Hutchinson family loses two daughters to the Plague

1634 Anne and William and their children emigrate to the Massachusetts Bay Colony to follow Reverend John Cotton

1636 Roger Williams is banished and founds Rhode Island

1636 Founding of Harvard College

1637 (May) Anne Hutchinson's friend and supporter Sir Henry Vane loses the governorship to John Winthrop

1637 (November) Civil trial of Anne Hutchinson

1637-38 Winter of Anne's imprisonment

1638 (March) Ecclesiastical trial and final banishment of Anne Hutchinson; her family and several supporters move to Rhode Island

1642 Death of William Hutchinson; Anne Hutchinson, concerned that the Massachusetts Bay Colony may take over Rhode Island, moves to the more

liberal Dutch colony; settles north of New
Amsterdam

1643   Increasing hostilities between the Dutch and the
local Indians

1643 (September) Anne Hutchinson's household is
attacked and burned; all present are killed except
for Susannah who is taken by the Siwanoy Indians

1645 (approximately) Susannah is returned to her family

1651 (December) Susannah Hutchinson marries John
Cole

1922   Statue of Anne Hutchinson is erected in front of
the Massachusetts State House in Boston

1945   Massachusetts state legislature revokes the
banishment order

1987   Massachusetts Governor Michael Dukakis
pardons Anne Hutchinson

2005   The 1922 statue of Anne Hutchinson is finally
officially dedicated

What Happened Next

Young Susannah Hutchinson lived for a few years with the Algonquian-speaking Siwanoy Indians before she was ransomed and returned to her surviving relatives. She married into one of the families that had opposed her mother.

Reverend John Cotton continued to slide safely between all theological differences and stay in favor with the authorities.

Governor John Winthrop spent much of the remaining six years of his life writing about and justifying his regime.

Reverend Wilson remained minister of the First Church of Boston until his death in old age.

Anne's brother-in-law John Wheelwright returned to Boston and was forgiven.

Mary Dyer eventually became a Quaker and many years later was hanged in Boston.

Also:

The Hutchinson River Parkway, north of New York City, has frequent traffic jams of people who know nothing about Anne Hutchinson. Locals refer to the parkway with some affection as "The Hutch." The split rock is still there, not far from the even busier lanes of I-95.

The Pequot Indians, almost wiped out by the forces of the Massachusetts Bay Colony, are now the richest Native American group in the United States, thanks to their highly successful casino.

The Antinomians were a splinter sect in sixteenth-century Germany who, believing that virtue was no proof of grace, felt free to act however they wished. To call Anne Hutchinson an Antinomian was therefore to label her immoral. *Antinomian* became a bugaboo term like *Communist* during the Cold War or *Secular Humanist* in a time of religious fervor.

Rumor has it that Harvard still struggles with political correctness.

And many people in this country and elsewhere are still trying to make smart, passionate women hold their tongues.

A Gynecological Note

Anne Hutchinson's "monstrous birth" in Rhode Island has now been diagnosed as what is called a hydatiform mole or a molar pregnancy. In these cases the mass consists of out-of-control placental material. The uterus is overly enlarged for the apparent month of the pregnancy, and frequently there is no fetus present. Instead, the tissue takes a grape-like form which can be clearly seen when the pieces leave the uterus.

This developmental disorder occurs in approximately 1 out of 1500 pregnancies, and women over 40 have a higher incidence. Risk factors can include diets low in protein and other nutritional elements, a likely scenario for Anne both before and during her imprisonment.

Mary Dyer's "monster" has received less medical attention, probably in part because the circumstances of its revelation invited exaggeration and devil-like comparisons rather than reliable fact. Nevertheless, the general consensus has been that her still-born was anencephalic, that is, without a fully-developed brain. There has also been some internet speculation that the description—minus spines, talons, and horns—might suggest imperfectly differentiated Siamese twins.

In each case, of course, gynecological misfortune was seen by the Puritan authorities as the judgment of God falling upon a sinning woman.

A Final Comment

In retrospect, it is not surprising that conformist Boston of the 1630's was sent into a tailspin by Anne Hutchinson. A medieval mystic, she was too intensely spiritual for the Puritans; a modern activist, she violated all Biblical injunctions intended to keep women down.

It was not just religious hair-splitting that made her such a problem for Governor Winthrop and his cronies. What drove them crazy was her great skill at theological debate combined with her easy disregard for their patriarchal authority. She was condemned as a heretic but really she was banished for threatening the absolute dominance of the (male) civil government.

In the tradition of Puritan Boston, people in this country are still trying to control the expression of ideas with which they disagree.

And one more point: when I think about Anne's story, I am impressed with her husband. While Winthrop called William Hutchinson *"a man of weak parts and wholly influenced by his wife,"* it seems to me that William can also be seen as a man who was confident enough not to be threatened by his wife's prominence. Sexual intimacy within marriage was seen as desirable by the Puritans, and perhaps Anne and William's close physical bond strengthened them both.

Works Consulted

Note:

All quoted material is italicized. In the interests of
readability I have felt free to modernize or condense the
language of my seventeenth-century sources. I have not
fundamentally altered any text.

We are fortunate that so many of Anne Hutchinson's
words have been preserved. One way to be
immortalized is to be sufficiently annoying.

Crawford, Deborah, *Four Women in a Violent Time*, Crown,
New York, 1970

Dunn, Richard S. and Laetitia Yeandle, Editors, *The
Journal of John Winthrop, 1630-1649,* The Belknap Press of
Harvard University Press, Cambridge, Massachusetts,
1996

Gordon, Charlotte, *Mistress Bradstreet: The Untold Life of
America's First Poet,* Little, Brown and Company, New
York, New York, 2005

Hall, David D., Editor, *The Antinomian Controversy, 1636-
1638: A Documentary History,* Duke University Press,
Durham, North Carolina, 2nd edition 1990

Howe, Susan, *The Birth-Mark: Unsettling the Wilderness in
American Literary History*, Wesleyan University Press,
University Press of New England, Hanover, New
Hampshire, 1993

Johnson, Edward, *Wonder-Working Providence of Sions Savior
in New-England,* 1654. Reprint, Delmar, New York:

Scholars Facsimile and Reprints, 1974

Jones, Howard Mumford and Bessie Zaban, *The Many Voices of Boston: A Historical Anthology 1630-1975*, Little, Brown, and Company, Boston, 1975

Kamensky, Jane, *Governing the Tongue: The Politics of Speech in Early New England*, Oxford University Press, New York, 1997

Karlsen, Carol F., *The Devil in the Shape of a Woman: Witchcraft in Colonial New England*, Norton, New York, 1987

Kirkpatrick, Katherine, *Trouble's Daughter: The Story of Susanna Hutchinson, Indian Captive*, Delacorte Press, New York, 1998

LaPlante, Eve, *American Jezebel: The Uncommon Life of Anne Hutchinson, The Woman who Defied the Puritans*, HarperCollins, New York, 2004

Leonardo, Bianca and Winifred K. Rugg, *Anne Hutchinson: Unsung Heroine of History*, Tree of Life Publications, Joshua Tree, California, 1995

Mattis, Emery, *Saints and Sectaries: Anne Hutchinson and the Antinomian Controversy in the Massachusetts Bay Colony*, University of North Carolina Press, Chapel Hill, North Carolina, 1962

Nichols, Joan Kane, *A Matter of Conscience: The Trial of Anne Hutchinson*, Raintree Steck-Vaughn Publishers, Austin, Texas, 1993

Rugg, Winifred, *Unafraid: A Life of Anne Hutchinson*, Ayer Company, Freeport, New York, 1930

Rutman, Darrett B., *Winthrop's Boston: Portrait of a Puritan Town 1630-1649*, University of North Carolina Press, Chapel Hill, North Carolina, 1965

Williams, Selma R., *Divine Rebel: The Life of Anne Marbury Hutchinson*, Holt, Rinehart and Winston, New York, 1981

http://www-medlib.med.utah.edu

http://www.annehutchinson.com

Printed in the United States
84487LV00005B/379-450/A